Gloucester is the Sea

With the compliments of the
author,
Miriam Selker Dodek

Gloucester is the Sea

and other poems of people, ocean and shore

Miriam Selker Dodek

EPM PUBLICATIONS, INC.

Library of Congress Cataloging in Publication Data
PS3554.033G5 811'.5'4 75-12826
ISBN: 0-914440-09-8

EPM Publications, Inc., 1003 Turkey Run Road, McLean, Va. 22101
(Distributed by Hawthorn Books)
Printed in the United States of America

Design by Anne Hanger

To my husband

Contents

The Face of Gloucester

In Gloucester, what you see
Depends upon a peculiarity:
What your hands engage in,
The paths your feet explore,
And what draws you to this town of earth's water door?
Do you live inland, inside the town, or near the shore?
Do you paint flowers, or grow them from seed,
Or raise vegetables because that is your need?
Do you sail on the ocean?
Or row in a fresh water pond,
Or lie on a sandy beach picturing lands beyond?
Or do you walk with a pen, or a brush in your hand,
To preserve for yourself the shape and color of the land?
Or do you fish for a living
And on each return whisper thanksgiving?

Gloucester turns to you the face you give her,
And all those you pass here, unknown, or unique in their fame,
Are all of us: we each do the same.

The Green-Glass Wall

The liquid green-glass wall
Rises up from nowhere,
Arrow line across the horizon,
Hangs motionless
A space moment . . .
Then sways in precarious balance . . .
Pauses . . . to shudder
Quiet gleaming menace
From its silver-topped frost;
It widens and thickens . . . it stirs,
Is born!
Wave in storm!

It leans forward
In translucent threat,
Bends ponderous towards the shore,
Glides slow, slow,
Faster, faster, through low growl
Of heavy water,
Drawing a hypnotic veil of green
Over the restless sea,
To magic swiftly, like Moses' staff,
Into curving serpent
Sliding on its glistening water belly,
With blind, green sight,
Advancing towards the craggy shore
Where the towering boulders guard the land
And wait, mustering all their age-old strength . . .
And now they stab and pierce the serpent . . .
The green tail lashes back in anger
With exploding whites,
Frantic circles of foam!

The indomitable rocks split
The monster to curling segments,

But one escapes the gray defenders,
Spits and spews watery claws
To crush the boulders,
To demolish them . . .
But then the paling segment gasps an ugly gasp,
Writhes . . . wanes . . . coiling ropes
Twisting lower and lower . . . falling helpless, inert.

The green serpent spatters
Into watery milk glass slivers,
Dies in the crevices of the unchanging rocks,
And in the empty shells scattered on the sand.

Wave in storm!
Birth, battle, terror,
And defeat.

Prayer of the Fishermen

The fishermen pray before they go out,
The fishermen pray before they set sail:
  "Close to the earth,
  Close to the sea,
  Close to the sky,
  The wind and Thee!

  "We are one with the earth,
  The moon, stars, fish in the sea,
  With storm, rain and wind
  That all come from Thee!

  "When wind and sea pull
  Down our boats
  Deep in the smashing trough
  Of waves, cold, high and pointed,
  Have mercy, oh Lord, have mercy,
  Are we not also Thine anointed?"

The Fisherman's Wife

The ever-changing skies,
The horizon,
The harbor
Fill the eyes
Of the fisherman's wife:
Will it rain?
Will it storm?
Is he safe?
The weather is her life.

The Lost Fishermen

There must be more to this vast scene
Of moving water than the idle, restless swells
Off shore would seem to mean:
Could it be that a soul
Lost at sea, suffocated in liquid air,
Springs to living breath
Beneath the waves,
In secret resurrection from death?

All those little waves foaming on to the shore,
Is someone hidden underneath,
Someone pushing them before?
They run on night and day,
Swift and sure in their course,
Who propels them on their paths
With continuous unending force?

I see the manes of white horses galloping,
Are there riders who urge them on?
Each leaps forward speedier than the other,
Could one be a father,
Another a brother?

Small Catch at Town Landing

On the tiny dock
Right off the boat
I passed a tin pail
Of water; in it
Small golden fish sparkled afloat.
They darted quick
With pert swish of tail,
Dashing round and across
Their watery jail!
But one, eager and fast,
Leaped up and up,
Straining to arch over the brim
In a desperate spurt,
I watched him
Slam hard on the pavement,
I knew he was hurt,
He flapped gold-thread fins futilely
On the rough, dry stone,
But out of his sea,
He died, struggling, alone.

The Sea People

Quickly the tide skips
On to the salt marsh,
Inward to the breeding ground
Of the Sea People.

The sea feeds its own,
The starfish, the eels, the frogs
Clinging to decaying logs,
The oysters, the clams, the snails
Floating around the sluggish bogs.

They feed greedily
In the sea's sustaining tide,
And afterwards, they romp
And dive and hide.

House on Bass Rocks

The house built high on Bass Rocks
Juts out into the sea,
Unknowing that night and day
The desiring waves at waters' edge
Nuzzle at its strength,
Seeking through the long heavy hours,
To find a crevice for its restless, searching fingers
To fit into, to hang on to, a foothold
To undermine the rock ledge,
To whittle out the house,
To send it crashing into the sea.

The Rocking Stones

On Bass Rocks Ledge
The rocking stones
Roll back and forth,
Click and click,
Sharp and harsh.
The greedy, seeking waves
Reach out for them
With watery hands;
Again and again they flee,
They roll from side to side,
They knock each other;
The sucking waves circle
Warily, warily around them,
Finally to retreat with the tide.
But the sea can bide its time. Now
The sun glistens on the stones' wet, pitted backs
As they tap each other gently.

One Lone Brown Goose

I know when the scarlet fall begins
To draw his first full breath,
And bright summer languishes,
Wails, and struggles to her death;
Then the one lone brown goose appears
With the white gulls outside on my own cove,
And honks to me through the window
That his northern home grows cold,
And it is time for him to rove
Over the sea to warmer land.
Next day over the water I see
Him rise into the sky
Strewn with his brown-wedged band
Veering south. Each year
He brings the calendar to me:
Fiery autumn, nights of winter,
Dawn of spring, a gladdening prophecy.

What Army?

What army can march
Straight as an ocean wave?
What army can stretch out
As even, and together,
Over the long, wide water?
Your eye cannot catch the end of it
Along with the beginning.
Does God measure out
The matching width of sky and air and wave?
That dread line of equal height
Further even than where the sky meets earth?
Or the steady, relentless width
The pushing tide makes
In the breathful moment
When that liquid wall breaks?
Does He?

Derelict

Once you saw schooners
Blow into the harbor
Under full sail,
There are no·more fairy tale
Ships now for waiting fishermen
To hail . . .
You can see one derelict ship
Floating there
Outside the harbor:
It staggers like an old man
Confused, lost.
The grayish veil,
A tattered dun sail,
Blurs his eyes,
But then the wind shifts,
The shredded sails lift,
The old one straightens
For a moment—until
The wind dies,
You can almost see that helpless
Panic in his rheumy eyes;
The ship wheels, flounders,
The waves slosh his elegy
And slap the decks,
Bobbing the derelict
Up and down, helpless, bereft,
Out to the open sea.

Sea Spawn

I could have been flung from the sea,
Unnumbered ages ago,
When the birth seed of the first dawn
Quickened scarlet on the ocean below
And spread its passionate light
Over the reluctant waters
And the resisting night.

At each dawning, uncertain remembrances
Press upon me,
Hesitate and linger,
Misting my memory
As I search for the key
To this mystical sequence
Of distant oceans, voices I can barely hear,
And odd, gurgling creatures
That slip by me to swim
On without fear,
And ages, long forgotten, explode dim
And far away, like the echo of the echo of a tolling bell
Muffled by the dark waters of a bottomless well.

And as the pursuing sun descends
To encompass and ravish the night,
I begin to know
I am kin of the sea and the dawn,
I begin to know I am
Their sea spawn!

Sea Gull

On the dock he gobbles dead fish entrails
The fishermen discard from their barrels
Underneath the boats' furled sails.
Then, with flat, wide-sieved beak pushed forward,
He straddles
On the boards of the dock to seek more,
And finally ends searching the shore,
Lifting up comic, orange paddles
At the end of each skinny leg.
I beg
Of you, recall him only in flight,
Else he is a grotesque sight,
For only when his white wings
Fleet across the sky,
Does the sea gull aesthetically satisfy.

Visitor by the Sea

She washed out her gloves
Every night,
Wrung out her hose
Tight and bright,
Her slip, her panties,
Her yellow dress,
Then mended and sorted
The ones to press;
The fragrant night sped swiftly by
Without a cry,
Without a sigh,
The stars came out,
Cloud sea over sea
Floated about,
But no eyes for the night,
No eyes for the moon,
She always had those little things
To do up in her room.

Thin Rain on the Shore

In the night
The thin rain pours down
In straight, birchtree lines
Outside my open window,
The virile outpouring to the ground,
The waves' strengthy, satisfying sound
Comforts me,
Quilt-embraced in my bed,
The rain beats on the earth
In relentless copulation,
I am the earth, loved, seeded, warm.

The Heart Beats Time

The sun comes up and the sun goes down,
And a day has lingered and reluctantly gone,
The stars fade sadly and the moon dims slow,
And there is another dawn, and another day will go:
But eve and dawn and setting sun
Leave no arabesques on the sand by the sea,
No trace by the beating waves is echoed,
And time lives only in the heart of me.

Widow's Walk

The house was quiet
Now, but she frowned
At the senseless, twilight riot
Of the gulls screaming overhead.

The day had been no worse
And no better,
She always tried to immerse
Her fears in the cleaning and washing and sewing,
Yet all the time knowing
He should be back by now.
It was like being strung on a rack
She once saw in a book.
She rose, climbed the narrow stair
And paused a moment there
To listen to her children's breathing;
They slept content in bed,
Bathed, loved, amply fed . . .
Nothing troubles them, she thought
Resentful, then felt guilty . . . *But they ought*
To laugh and play . . .
Still . . . their easy laughter mocked
Her loneness through the day.
Climbing the second stair to the Widow's Walk,
She went over what she'd say
When he came home. He was a silent man,
But they had good talk
When they sat together:
The boat, the catch, the church,
New holes in the net, the weather . . .
He was two months past due,
And he'd said he was set on just five

In all . . . if only she knew
He was safe and alive!
The waiting two months had taken
Roundness from her face, her eyes did not shine
And her food left a taste in her mouth
Like rancid wine.

Last time he was home, on the Widow's Walk
He painted the railings white as chalk,
And they striped her black skirt
Like a repeating buoy's flashing alert.
Sudden . . . the premonition of a wreck . . .
She loosened the scarf
The wind blew tight around her neck.
Maybe he was in a storm . . . maybe he is dead!
There was one on the Banks, the newspaper read.
She walked faster and faster,
Oh, what was a ship and a crew
Without its master?
She started, then turned her face away
As her neighbor shouted from her Widow's Walk,
What was there for her to say?
She wanted only husband-talk.
Over the gulls' cries the words, what did she shout?
"Home," she heard, "home!"
Quick as a shot, she turned about,
"They're due in tomorrow!"
. . . It was as if another, not she had felt the sorrow,
For swiftly it lifted and shifted from her, past the shore,
Oh, Angelo, if you return, I will not ask
The good Lord for anything more.

The grim day, past, was flooded with sun,
The grey night turned to silver,
The enemy ocean was now her friend,
Tomorrow these days and nights would end.

Voice of the Newborn

In my yard there seemed to be some babies crying,
They sounded very young, very rawkish,
I looked up
And saw the sea gulls flying
Low and wavering, clumsy, mawkish:
They were crying
Like the newborn, on and on,
And others joined them in reply
Like a mother talking, talking
Them to quiet,
But the rasping only heightened,
And they flew more swiftly,
They seemed frightened.
Their shrill, high screams
Pierced my house every night,
But this is not a similar flight:
I can feel the hovering alarm.
Is there threat of harm
That forces them to flee?
Perhaps a hawk or some killer bird
I cannot see.
I recognize the note they use
To call one another
No more than that.
But then, it's mostly language
That isolates a man from his brother.
Yet I would like to know why
They cry forlorn,
On this night
In the rasping voice of the newborn?

Gloucester is the Sea

Gloucester is the sea!
It lightens the spirit,
It joys the eyes,
It wings the mind
With imaginings
One could not
Otherwise find.

Above him the limitless sky,
His face turned to the sea,
His feet secure on the rocky coast,
A man can feel then, almost
A god,
Nourished by these three.

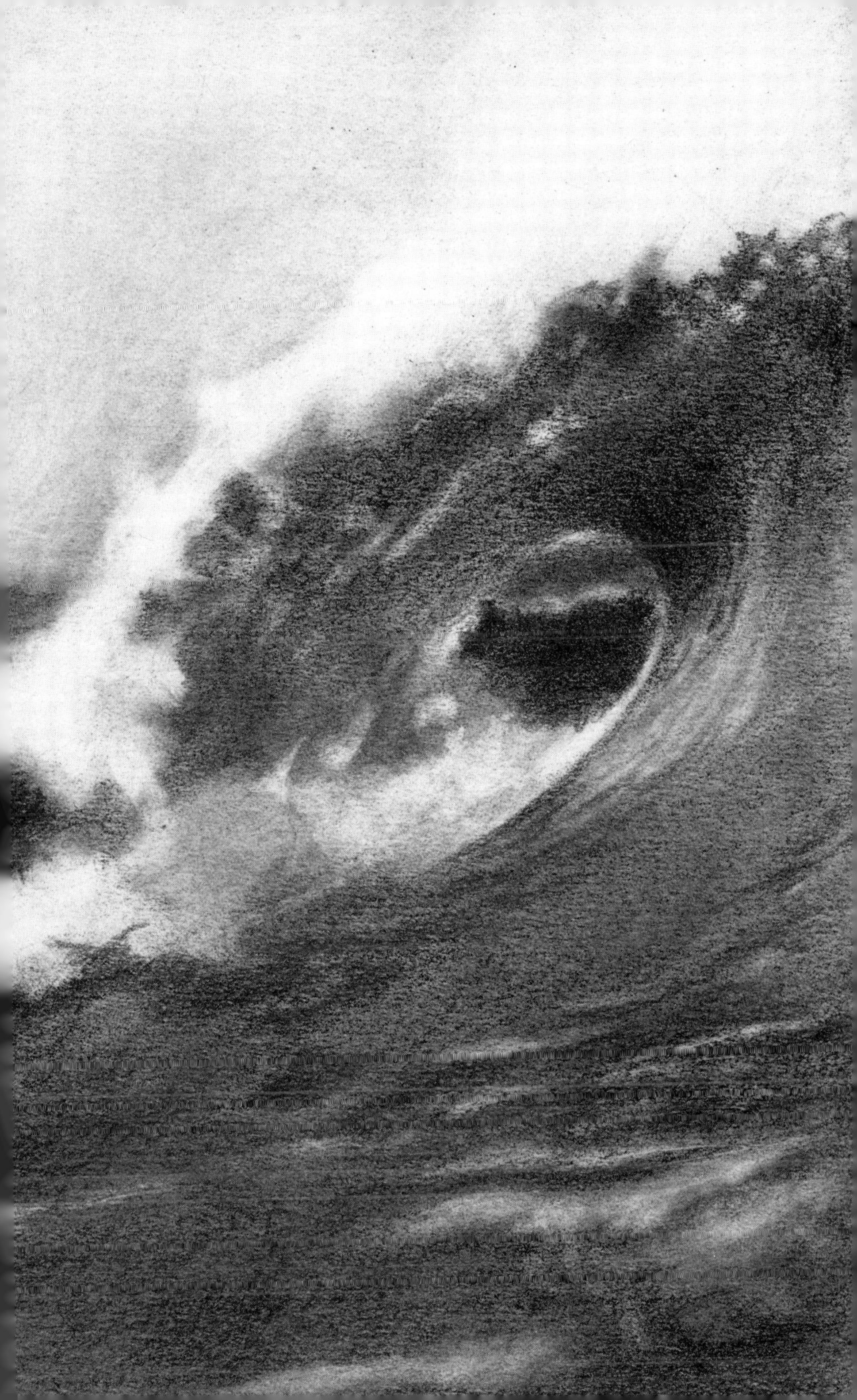

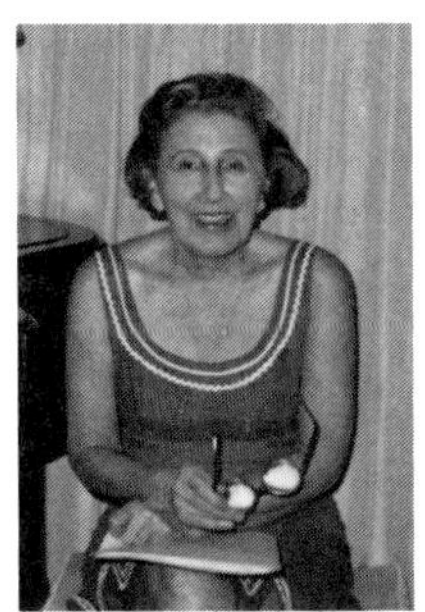

About the Author

Miriam Selker Dodek is the author of RIVER OF WONDERS, Stories of the Nile. Her short stories, book reviews, plays and poems have been published in many national magazines, including *American Poet, Opinion,* and *Reflex.* She has written and performed in two series of radio programs, WORLD OF THE POET and THE GOLDEN GODS, broadcast in the Washington, D.C. area. She read her poetry in a television special on NBC. In 1973 some of the poems in this volume were written and performed for a concert given by the Cape Ann Symphony Orchestra to honor the 350th anniversary of Gloucester's founding.

Born in Detroit, Mrs. Dodek attended Cleveland Heights High School in Cleveland. She was graduated from the University of Michigan with honors in English Literature and received her M.A. from Western Reserve University. She has a doctorate from Northwestern University Law School. A former attorney for the federal government in Washington, she lives there now with her husband, Dr. Samuel M. Dodek, a physician. They have two daughters.

The Dodeks have had their summer home in Bass Rocks, Gloucester, Massachusetts, for many years. Mrs. Dodek says she comes back to it, after her travels, with anticipation and peace in her heart. She loves the sea and finds it a perfect companion. Her poems tell that story.